ICELANDIC
MAGIC
FOR
MODERN
LIVING

Andrews McMeel Publishing
a division of Andrews McMeel Universal
1130 Walnut Street, Kansas City, Missouri 64106

www.andrewsmcmeel.com

17 18 19 20 21 SDB 10 9 8 7 6 5 4 3 2 1

ISBN: 978-1-4494-8977-9

Library of Congress Control Number: 2017951693

Editor: Allison Adler
Graphic Illustrations: Habba Nero
Layout and Design: Ragnar Helgi Ólafsson
Art Director: Tim Lynch
Production Editor: David Shaw
Production Manager: Cliff Koehler

ATTENTION: SCHOOLS AND BUSINESSES

Andrews McMeel books are available at quantity discounts with bulk purchase for educational, business, or sales promotional use. For information, please e-mail the Andrews McMeel Publishing Special Sales Department: specialsales@amuniversal.com.

BOFF KONKERZ

Icelandic
Magic

FOR

Modern
Living

Andrews McMeel
PUBLISHING®

In the beginning ...

It was a dark and stormy summer's night in the West-fjords when famed Icelandic archaeologist Ruglukollur Gottskálksson discovered an old wooden trunk buried beneath the floorboards of a deserted church 10 miles west of Breiðavík. The trunk contained hitherto unknown illustrations and text credited to the legendary "Icelandic Nostradamus." Skáldsögn Skáldskapardóttir. Ruglukollur found over a hundred previously unseen magical symbols or "staves." Each stave was drawn along with a corresponding spell to trigger its effects. Most surprising of all was that the staves related not to the 1600's, when they were written down, but to life in the first decades of the 21st century! Contained within this book are a selection of those precognitive magical symbols, along with the spells and rituals that give them their power. Readers are advised to approach the claims of this powerful and ancient sorcery with extreme caution as the spells themselves are sometimes dangerous to perform and their effects are not guaranteed.

STAVE 1

Sorgmæddi beinirinn

Stave for fast Wifi

Take your router and carve this stave onto it using the tip of a narwhal tusk. Place the router in a bucket and fill the bucket with Brennivín.* Leave the router soaking in the bucket for twenty four hours. Your Wifi will always be super-fast and your house will smell of caraway.

STAVE 2

Skruddustafur

*Stave for more friends
on Facebook*

Write this stave on the inside of a hen's egg without breaking the shell. Place this egg inside a well-worn sock and hide the sock inside a living cat belonging to a blind fishmonger. You will have more friends.

STAVE 3

Rasshausastafur

Necrohat stave

Two friends make an agreement that when one of them dies the other will flay his buttocks and make a hat from the skin. The living friend will then put this stave under the hat and place it on his head. The hat will fuse with the scalp of the wearer and whatever bar he enters there will always be happy hour. If the wearer of the hat dies while the hat is fused to his head his soul will never find peace and will wander Laugavegur* in search of a happy hour for all eternity. The only way to remove the hat is by persuading someone to listen to fourteen hours of terrible hip-hop. When the fourteen hours are up the wearer can remove the hat and give it to the new owner, who will now find cheap drinks wherever he wanders.

STAVE 4

Skjóttgrafarstafur

*Stave to always lead you back
to Dunkin Donuts*

Buy one hundred assorted donuts from Dunkin Donuts and eat ninety nine of them. Take the remaining donut and place it on the grave of an orphan who died from a broken heart. Run around the grave counterclockwise seven-ty two times and then feed the donut to a three legged dog. No matter where in the world you are, you will always find your way back to Dunkin Donuts.

STAVE 5

Skyldmennastafur

*Stave to avoid sleeping
with your cousin*

Carve this stave on a piece of harðfiskur* the size of your palm. Coat the carved stave with a mixture of sour milk and selur.* Place the harðfiskur in your underwear and leave there until it becomes one with your skin. You will not sleep with your cousin (or anyone else).

STAVE 6

Grísastafur

*Stave to be rid of
a corrupt politician*

Carve this stave onto the last piece of cake. Place the cake outside the government building. The greedy politician will come running to eat the last piece of cake, when he/she arrives, throw bananas at him/her until he/she resigns.

WARNING: Once the corrupt politician has been made to resign he/she will simply appoint another corrupt politician to replace him/her, therefore this spell must be repeated often.

STAVE 7

Blekkingarstafur

Stave to release your
inner "viking"

Paint this stave on the prow of your longship (car) with the blood of your fallen foes (red paint). Drink very expensive authentic viking beer, grow a viking beard, watch shows on your genuine viking TV where half naked men shout and wave swords about. Shout and wave a sword about yourself. Wear an authentic plastic viking helmet with horns. Wander around Laugavegur* at 3am wondering where all your money and friends have gone.

You're a viking! Grrrrr.....

STAVE 8

Greddustafur

*Stave to become
a hit on Tinder*

Have this stave tattooed on your ass. Use a picture of the tattoo as your main picture on Tinder. Remove your dignity with a rusty shoehorn. Lower your standards.

Congratulations, you are now popular.

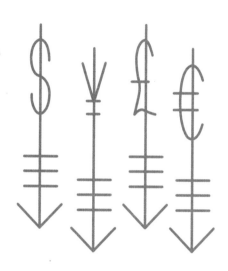

STAVE 9

Hrunstafur

*Stave to bring about
an economic collapse*

Carve this stave into the foundations of a hotel under construction in downtown Reykjavík. Make sure that the hotel is being built with borrowed money. By the time the hotel is completed the tourist bubble will have burst and the hotel owners will not be able to pay the banks the money they owe them. So much money will have been invested in the fickle business of tourism that the economy will fail.

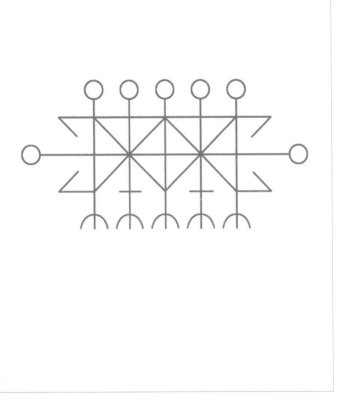

STAVE 10

Snáfiðistafur

Stave to get rid of tourists

Scratch this stave onto nine cranes in the downtown Reykjavík area with a humpback whale tooth. In no time at all 101* will be turned into one big construction site, most stores will become foreign fast food outlets, most apartments available for rent will be rented out to tourists by the night making downtown unaffordable for local people. Eventually Reykjavík will lose the very thing that made it attractive to tourists in the first place and they will stay away.

STAVE 11

Tælingarstafur

Stave to bring in tourists

Scratch this stave onto nine humpback whales in the downtown Reykjavík area with a piece of metal pulled from a crane. In no time at all 101* will be turned into one big construction site, most stores will become foreign fast food outlets, most apartments available for rent will be rented out to tourists by the night making downtown unaffordable for local people. Eventually Reykjavík will lose the very thing that made it attractive to tourists in the first place, but they'll keep coming anyway because they won't know any better.

STAVE 12

Stafastafur

*Stave to choose an Icelandic
magical stave for your next tattoo*

Steal a bible from a church and draw this stave on every page using a mixture of Mix* and puffin semen. Bury the bible fifty feet beneath the ocean floor and set it on fire; that night the stave you should get tattooed will be revealed to you in a dream.

It will be Vegvísir.*

STAVE 13

Kjaftæðisstafur

Stave to convince the world
you've had a revolution

Paint this stave onto your laptop and go online. Manu-facture and distribute a million memes and false news stories claiming that Iceland had a revolution and jailed 480,000 bankers for a total of 2,000,000 years. Make wild claims that after the protests in 2009 everyone in Iceland was cleared of debt and had their mortgages paid off. The world will believe these claims as most people believe anything they read online.

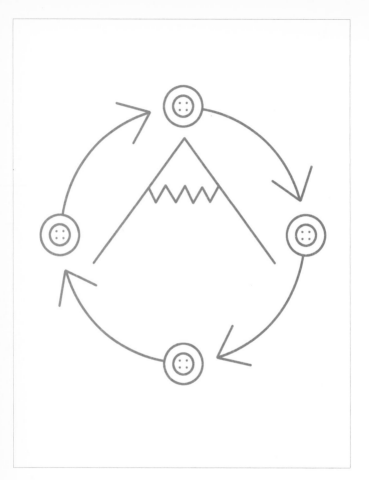

STAVE 14

Eyðileggingarstafur

*Stave to destroy natural
beauty spots*

Write this stave in invisible ink on a tourist guidebook. Promote your country's natural beauty spots hard in all forms of media. Provide busses to and from the natural beauty spots, build visitor centers and cafes, tourist shops and parking lots. Make a concerted effort to get as many people as possible to visit said spots, but do not allow the huge numbers of visitors to be present in any promotional photography. Eventually the very thing that made your natural wonders attractive in the first place will be gone, but on the plus side a small amount of people will have made a lot of money.

STAVE 15

Bobbingastafur

Stave to free the nipple

If you find yourself in a society where male and female nudity are treated differently, thanks to outdated sexual oppression and an inherent fear of the female body, you should paint this stave on the center of your chest, soak your bra in gasoline, set it on fire and cast it into the crater of an active volcano (be sure to remove the bra first). From this point onwards you and your wonderful life giving nipples will be free.

STAVE 16

Gnarrstafur

*Stave to get a comedian
elected as mayor*

Travel back in time to 2009. Carve this stave onto a DVD of Íslenski draumurinn* and place the disc beneath the left foot of the statue of Leifur Eiríksson* outside Hallgrímskirkja* while listening to "Penis Envy" on your Sony Walkman. A local comedian will be elected mayor of a large city in Iceland and save the world.

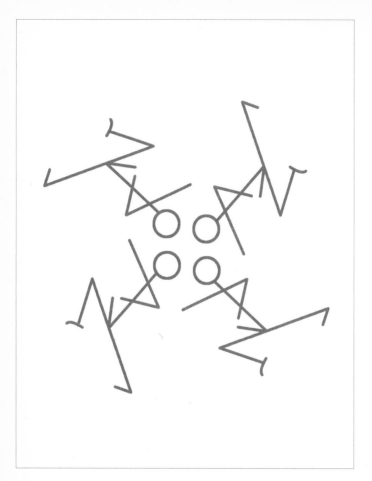

STAVE 17

Göndulstafur

Stave to get more action
on Grindr

Take a hammer and beat this stave onto the screen of your smartphone. Spend the next year visiting the gym at least 6 days per week, grow a beard to hide your weak chin and get both nipples pierced. Keep an eye on the latest men's fashion and dress accordingly. Work on your eyebrows (see TRÚÐASTAFUR, page 47) Visit the dentist regularly, pay close attention to personal hygiene and spend at least two weeks out of every three months sunning yourself in the Canary Islands. When your year is up create a new Grindr account. You will have more hot guy on guy action than you can shake a stick at.

STAVE 18

Hégómastafur

*Stave to get more likes
on Instagram*

To get more likes on Instagram, log out of your account at midnight on a moonless night, write this stave on your forehead with the blood of a depressed mouse and take a selfie in front of a poor widow's back door. Log back onto Instagram at dawn and post the selfie and your likes will multiply from that point onwards.

STAVE 19

Grænkustafur

*Stave to guarantee you'll see
the northern lights*

Paint the lenses of your sunglasses black and once it dries paint this stave on the lenses with green ink. Head out into nature on the longest day of the year and drink several large glasses of Jameson's and Mix.* Remove all of your clothes and throw them into the sea, down a hole or into an active volcano. Smoke a ridiculous amount of Cannabis sativa forma indica. Walk back into town wearing the magic sunglasses. Go directly to your home and google "aurora borealis." You will see the northern lights in all its glory.

STAVE 20

Trúðastafur

*Stave to have the
mightiest eyebrows*

Paint this stave on the back of your mirror with the tears of a sexually dominant herring. Steal a bottle of black ink from a handsome tattooist, pour the ink into half a coconut and sit in front of your mirror. Using only the backs of your hands shape and define your brows with the ink. Do not be shy; if you need to shave the front of your hair to have room to freely express your eyebrow based sense of self then do so. When the ink is dry take several selfies of your mighty brows and post to all available social media. Your brow game is strong. Your brows are on point. You are complete.

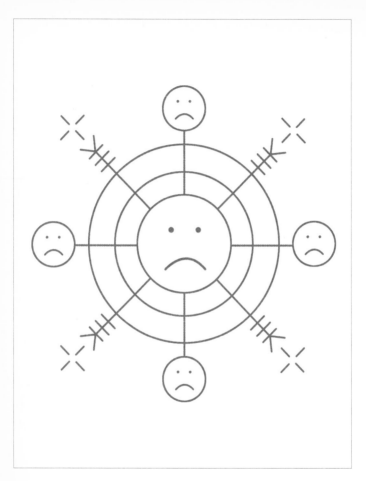

STAVE 21

Drullusokkastafur

*Stave to make your neighbor's
fireworks fail*

If you and your neighbor are sworn enemies you should
paint this stave on the underside of your neighbor's car
as he drives past on Christmas morning. On New Year's
Eve your neighbor's fireworks will splutter and fizz in a
pathetic parody of pyrotechnic splendor and the wailing
and lamentation of his children will be as music to your
ears.

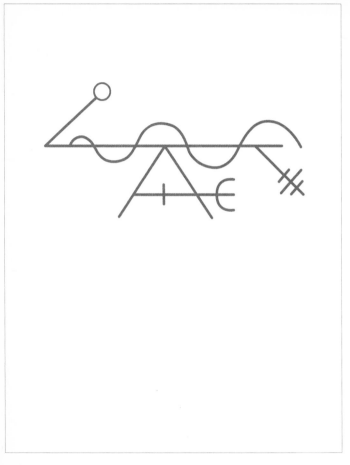

STAVE 22

Þöggunarstafur

*Stave to quiet
a bothersome child*

Take a piece of duct tape eight inches long. Draw this stave onto the tape using children's crayons while reciting the words "Bíum, bíum, bambaló, bambaló og dillidillidó."* Stick the tape securely across the bothersome child's mouth. Place the child in the trunk of your car. You will have peace and quiet.

STAVE 23

Skammstafur

Stave to see a whale

Carve this stave onto the sea with your left hand while walking backwards in a circle. Take the seawater with the stave carved on it and burn it in an ugly child's shoe. Go to a restaurant in downtown Reykjavík and order whale. Look at your plate – you have seen a whale in Iceland.

STAVE 24

Álfastafur

Stave to see hidden people

Tattoo this stave onto your forehead and travel to the Westfjords at midsummer. Wander off into the mountains alone. Consume half an ounce of dried psilocybe cubensis mushroom and nearly two ounces of Lysergic acid diethylamide.

You will see hidden folk.

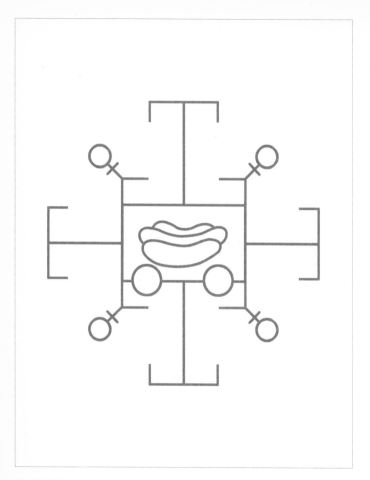

STAVE 25

Innmatarstafur

*Stave to turn a humble hot dog
stand into a national institution*

Paint this stave onto your belly with mustard and ketchup. World leaders and celebrities will flock to your hot dog wagon to stand by a freezing construction site chowing down on processed lips and arseholes served in a tasty bun. And no one will ever know why or understand the attraction.

STAVE 26

Bullstafur

*Stave to help an outlander
learn Icelandic*

Write this stave on the inside cover of a book on learning
Icelandic and throw it in the bin. If any outlander attempts
to speak a word of Icelandic do not try and understand
them, either switch to English or look bewildered. If the
outlander pronounces a word 95% correct then focus in on
the 5% that is incorrect and shake your head in confusion.
If the outlander pronounces all the words correctly, but
you detect the hint of an accent switch immediately to
English. Make sure to laugh in glee every time a foreign
reporter tries and fails to pronounce vaðlaheiðarvegavinnuverkfærageymsluskúraútidyralyklakippuhringur.*

STAVE 27

Pissstafur

*Stave to help you eat
fermented hákarl**

Carve this stave onto your bladder with a rib from a living shark. Urinate into a glass and stand the glass on your windowsill. Wait several weeks until the urine has evaporated down to the last centimeter and is a dark orange in color, take the glass and drink the contents. Repeat this process several times. Eventually you will develop a taste for hákarl.

STAVE 28

Metsölustafur

*Stave to make your book
a bestseller*

Invent a selection of "Icelandic Magic for Modern Living." Credit these staves to an imaginary "Icelandic Nostradamus" character that you have invented. Print the book and offer it for sale at shops frequented by tourists in downtown Reykjavík. If you put this stave on the cover of your book, it will be a huge international bestseller and the basis for an Oscar-winning movie. You will be rich beyond your wildest dreams. Takk!

Endnotes

* Odd Icelandic things

101: Postal code for downtown Reykjavík, the place where the magic happens! Home to a plethora of shops, restaurants, bars and bewildered tourists wondering where all their money has gone. Also the densest concentration of noodle houses outside of Asia (with more to come!).

Bíum, bíum, bambaló, bambaló og dillidillidó: Old Icelandic nursery rhyme used to entertain children before the invention of smartphones.

Brennivín: Icelandic schnapps. Traditionally used to wash away the taste of fermented shark (the only thing that tastes worse than Brennivín).

Hallgrímskirkja: The big church on the hill.

Harðfiskur: Tasty dried fish. Eaten with butter, like bread. Also used as replacement soles for worn out shoes.

Hákarl: Shark, eaten fermented by gullible tourists. The shark has no kidneys, therefore the ammonia (piss) is distributed throughout the meat of the animal, resulting in it's "unique" flavor.

Íslenski draumurinn: The best Film about football and Iceland ever. Stars Jón Gnarr, then future mayor of Reykjavík. Cruely overlooked by the 2000 Oscars.

Laugavegur: Main thoroughfare through downtown Reykjavík and a great place to enjoy all things puFFin.

Leifur Eiríksson: Icelandic hero (see his statue manfully standing outside the big church on the hill) and first European to set foot on the North American continent.

Mix: Radioactive florescent green fizzy drink given to Icelandic children as a form of punishment.

Selur: Any of 32 species of web-footed aquatic mammals that live chiefly in cold seas and whose body shape, round at the middle and tapered at the ends, is adapted to swift and graceful swimming. Known in English as seal.

Vaðlaheiðarvegavinnuverkfærageymsluskúraútidyralyklakippuhringur: The longest Icelandic word with 64 letters. Literal translation: "A ring on a key chain for the main door of a tool storage shed used by road workers on the hill Vaðlaheiði." Probably a joke.

Vegvísir: Best known of all Icelandic magical staves. Most popular stave for tourists to get as a tattoo. The question is: do they choose Vegvísir, or does it choose them?

Illustration

MAKE YOUR OWN MAGIC STAVE